Ambulances

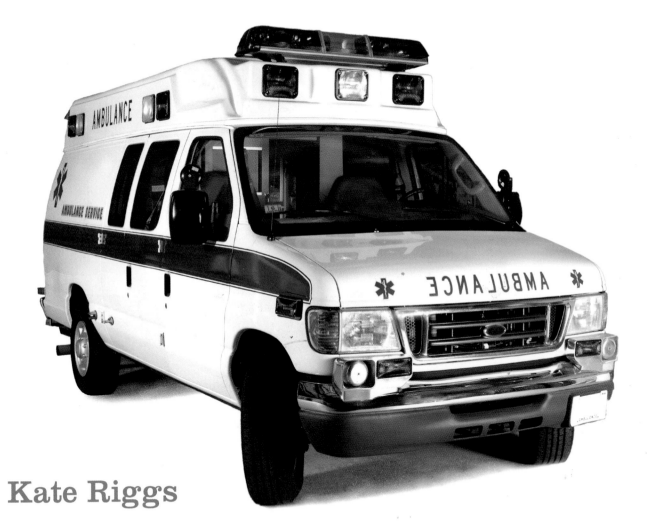

Kate Riggs

CREATIVE EDUCATION • CREATIVE PAPERBACKS

Published by Creative Education and Creative Paperbacks
P.O. Box 227, Mankato, Minnesota 56002
Creative Education and Creative Paperbacks
are imprints of The Creative Company
www.thecreativecompany.us

Design by Ellen Huber
Production by Travis Green
Art direction by Rita Marshall
Printed in Malaysia

Photographs by 123RF (welcomia), Corbis (Tetra Images),
Dreamstime (Bigjom, Brad Calkins, Carlosphotos, Colleen
Coombe, Denys Kurylow, Pavel Losevsky, Mrdoomits, Hongqi
Zhang [aka Michael Zhang]), Getty Images (Pat LaCroix,
Andrew Leyerle), iStockphoto (Foxtrot101, JSABBOTT,
lauradyoung, monkeybusinessimages), Shutterstock (Digital
Storm, jerrysa, travis manley, Leonid Smirnov)

Library of Congress Cataloging-in-Publication Data
Riggs, Kate.
Ambulances / Kate Riggs.
p. cm. — (Seedlings)
Includes bibliographical references and index.
Summary: A kindergarten-level introduction to ambulances,
covering their EMTs, equipment, role in rescuing, and such
defining features as their sirens.
ISBN 978-1-60818-578-8 (hardcover)
ISBN 978-1-62832-183-8 (pbk)
1. Ambulances—Juvenile literature. I. Title.

TL235.8.R54 2015
629.222'34—dc23   2014034713

CCSS: RI.K.1, 2, 3, 4, 5, 6, 7;
RI.1.1, 2, 3, 4, 5, 6, 7; RF.K.1, 3; RF.1.1

First Edition HC 9 8 7 6 5 4 3 2 1
First Edition PBK 9 8 7 6 5 4 3 2 1

TABLE OF CONTENTS

Time to Help! 5

Hospital Bound 6

Striped Trucks 8

Ambulance Alert 10

Working in Ambulances 13

Emergency Aid 14

Doctors and Nurses 17

Ready to Help! 18

Picture an Ambulance 20

Words to Know 22

Read More 23

Websites 23

Index 24

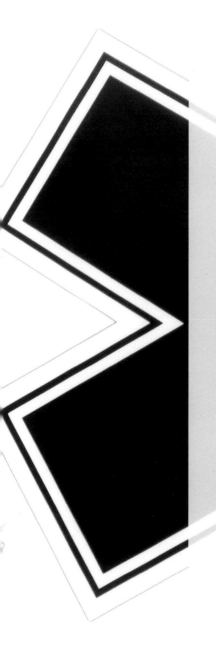
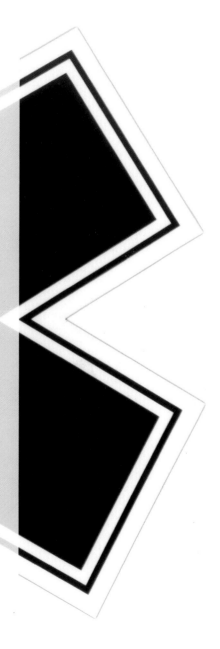

Time to help!

Ambulances help people who are hurt.

They take them
to the hospital.

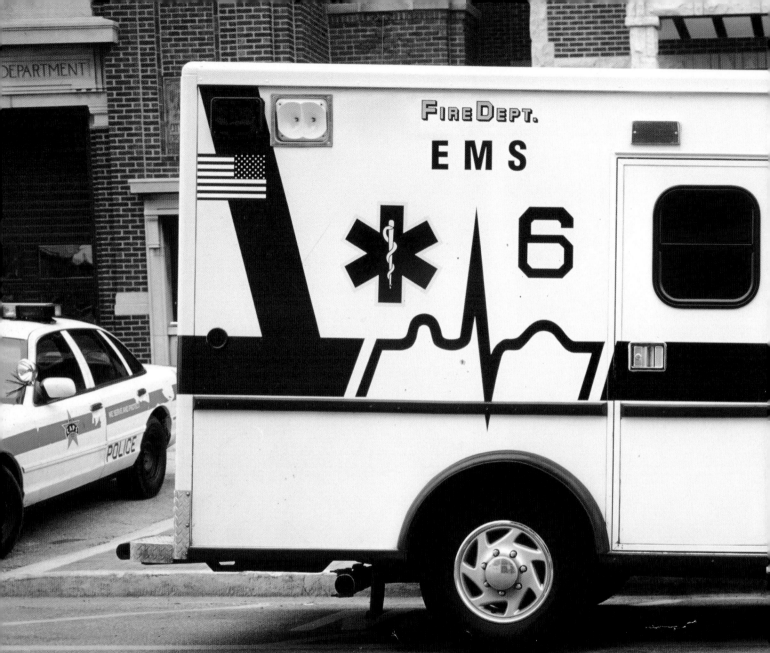

An ambulance looks
like a big van.

It is usually white.
It has stripes on the sides.

Ambulances have lots of flashing lights. They have noisy sirens, too.

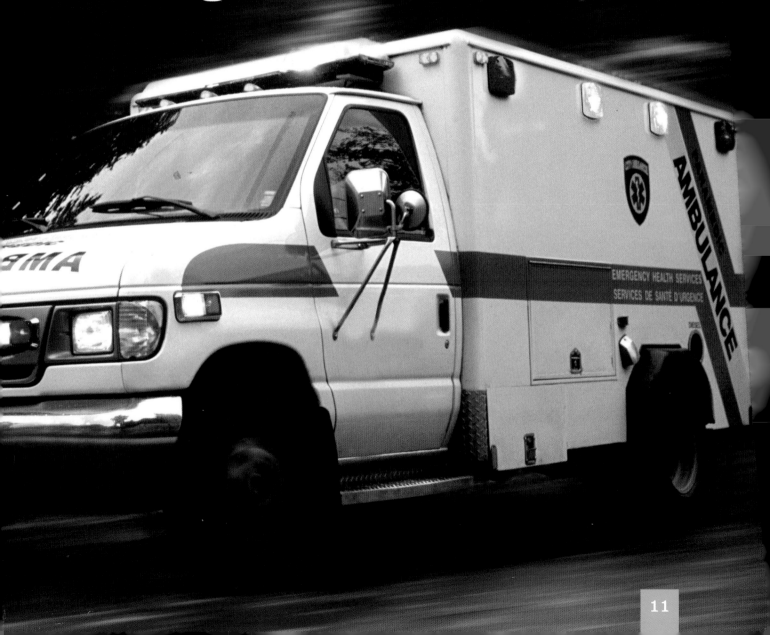

These tell people to get out of the way!

One person drives the ambulance. Other workers are called EMTs.

People in an emergency call an ambulance. EMTs use first aid. They put a hurt person on a stretcher.

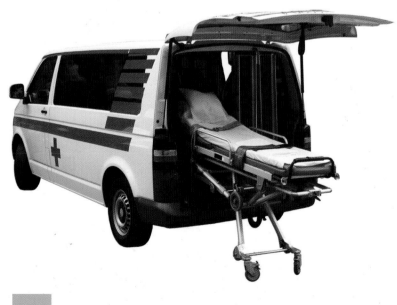

Doctors and nurses meet the EMTs. Then the ambulance goes back to its base.

Ready to help again!

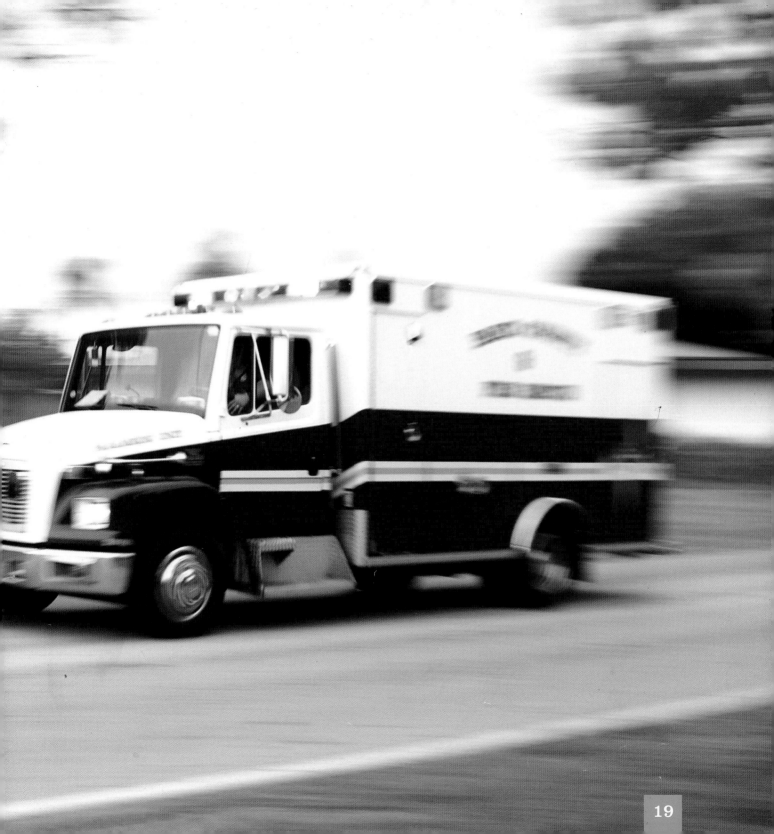

Picture an Ambulance

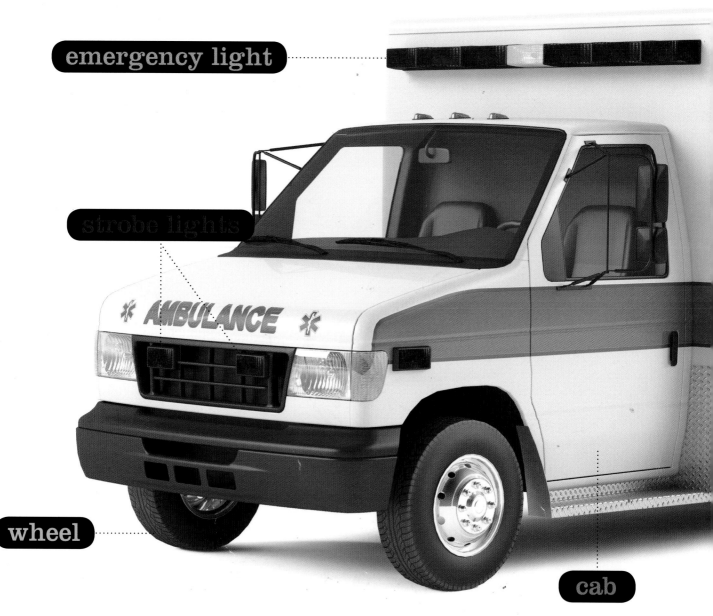

emergency light

strobe lights

wheel

cab

AMBULANCE

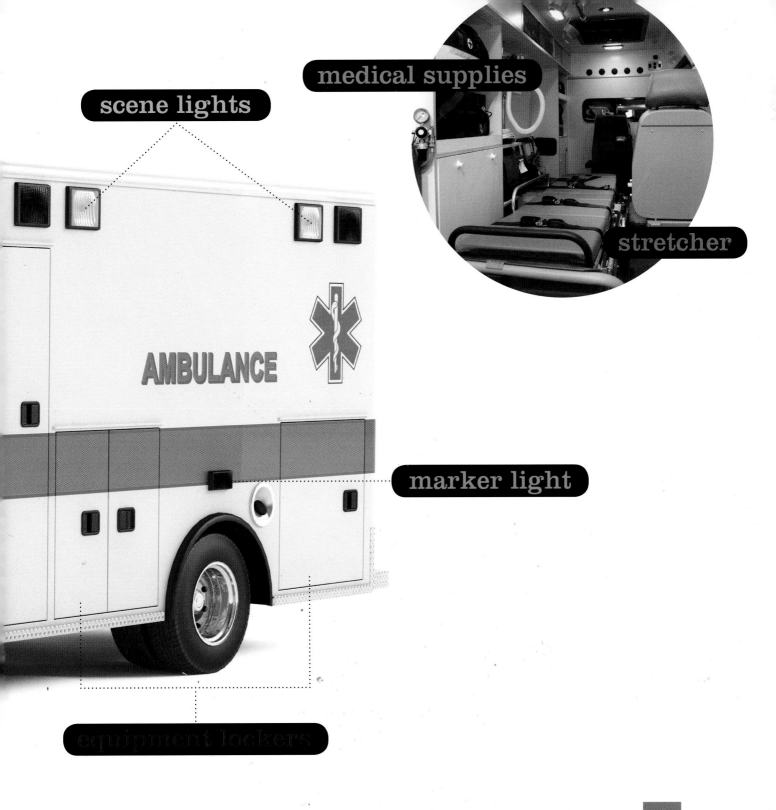

scene lights

medical supplies

stretcher

AMBULANCE

marker light

equipment lockers

Words to Know

emergency: something bad that happens suddenly

first aid: the first things you can do for someone who is hurt

hospital: the place where doctors and nurses work to help people heal

sirens: things that make loud noises as a sign that a vehicle is coming

stretcher: a special bed on wheels used in an ambulance or helicopter

Read More

Chancellor, Deborah. *Ambulance Rescue.*
Mankato, Minn.: Smart Apple Media, 2014.

Manolis, Kay. *Ambulances.*
Minneapolis: Bellwether Media, 2008.

Websites

DLTK's Transportation Coloring Pages
http://www.dltk-kids.com/crafts/transportation
/mtransposter.html
Click on the picture of the ambulance to print and color.

Emergency Vehicle Parking Game
http://www.primarygames.com/arcade/skill
/parkmyemergencyvehicle/
Try parking emergency vehicles like an ambulance!

Index

colors **9**

doctors **17**

drivers **13**

emergencies **14**

EMTs **13, 14, 17**

first aid **14**

hospitals **7**

lights **10**

nurses **17**

sirens **10**

stretchers **14**

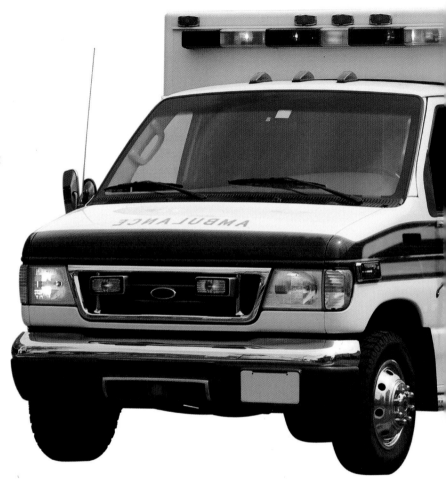